G R E A T

OYSTER ROCKS

Beacon
MOULINET

CASTLE
CORNET
Telegraph Post

CONTINUATION OF CAUSEWAY

COW
BAY

Opening required by Ordr Board

N.W. Angle

Tide Gauge

Steps

RING ROCK

CAUSEWAY TO CASTLE CORNET

TERRES POINT

SUNKEN ROCKS

SHINOLE

Boat Passage 60ft Wide

Tide & Mooringe ft

LA BOUE DE MORTE FEMME

VERMIERE
ROCK

EAST QUAY

Steps

DOCK
50 feet

ENTRANCE

BLANC BEC ROCKS

SOUTH
QUAY

SOUTH CORNET

Low Water Equinoctial Spring Tides

WHITE
STONE

NORTH QUAY

Moorings Beacon E

Anfre Beacon S

NAVELEE
ROCK

FLOATING ROCK

Area 10 / 5

Steps

SOUTH BEACH

Pest House

LES PERNEE

WEST QUAY

SLIPWAY

Engine Hse Contractors

LINE OF NEW SEWER

Boundary of States Property

R T

GUERNSEY HARBOUR
PLAN
of
THE HARBOUR AND ROADS
of
St PETER-PORT
GUERNSEY,
as surveyed in May 1854,
by
Messrs LYSTER & BRUMELL,
shewing
THE NEW HARBOUR WORKS,
NOW IN COURSE OF CONSTRUCTION
AND
THE COMPLETE DESIGN FOR THE SAME,
AS DESCRIBED
in
Mr RENDEL'S REPORTS,
of
18th Oct. 1854 and 18th May 1855.

NOTE.

The Low Water Datum, to which the Soundings are reduced
and the levels of the Rocks refer, is that of an Equinoctial
Spring Tide, which falls 37 Feet below the landing at the Head
of the South Pier, of the present Harbour, at or 30 Feet
below High Water of the same data.

Up to the points marked thus ✱ the Works are already executed.

GUERNSEY
THROUGH THE LENS

Front End Papers
Before the building of the New Harbour of
St. Peter Port in the 1850s, several plans were
considered by the States of Guernsey. Only
part of this plan was adopted. The survey was
carried out by Messrs. Lyster and Bramell in
May 1854. It shows the harbour works then
in course of construction 'and the complete
design for the same, as described in Mr. Rendel's
reports of the 18th October, 1854 and 18th
May, 1855'. An improved scheme was accepted
by the States in 1860.

Back End Papers
Map of Guernsey published in Berry's *History
of Guernsey* in 1815.

Members of the Guernsey Photographic Society enjoying an outing about 1904

GUERNSEY
THROUGH THE LENS
including
ALDERNEY, SARK, HERM
and JETHOU

Photographs taken before 1914

Compiled by

VICTOR COYSH and **CAREL TOMS**

PHILLIMORE

1978
Published by
PHILLIMORE & CO. LTD.,
London and Chichester
Head Office: Shopwyke Hall,
Chichester, Sussex, England

ISBN 0 85033 311 3

Printed in Great Britain by
UNWIN BROTHERS LIMITED
at The Gresham Press, Old Woking, Surrey
and bound by
THE NEWDIGATE PRESS LTD.,
at Book House, Dorking, Surrey

Dedicated to the memory of

Charles H. Toms

*and other photographers who operated
in the Guernsey Bailiwick and whose work
has given pleasure to so many*

ACKNOWLEDGMENTS

The variety and number of illustrations in this book are largely due to the unstinting assistance given to us by many organisations and individuals who gladly loaned their precious records in order that a wider audience could enjoy them.

Many were drawn from our own collections, but we are most grateful to the people who were willing to show us photographs from which we were able to select those which, in our opinion, were among the best.

We would like to thank the following owners of photographs for the loan of material to be used in this book: States of Guernsey Ancient Monuments Committee, Mr. Rex Birch, Mr. H. Capper, the Misses K. O. and N. A. Dennis, Miss R. de la Rue, Mr. A. S. Gould, Mr. Peter Girard, Mr. Alan Guppy, Mrs. Ingham, Mr. H. Lihou, Miss P. Webb, Mr. L. Quinain.

Some of our helpers deserve special mention: Mr. J. M. Y. Trotter, Librarian, Priaulx Library, for allowing photographs on file to be copied and the premises to be used as our headquarters; Miss Doris Cook, also of the Priaulx Library, for her unflagging assistance; Mr. Ernest Brett, Librarian, Guille-Allès Library, for allowing the library's photographic collections to be used; the Guernsey Press Co. Ltd., for permitting the use of previously published photographs.

CONTENTS

LIST OF ILLUSTRATIONS

INTRODUCTION

The 19th century was one of the most important eras in the history of the Guernsey Bailiwick. A great many public buildings were completed, including places of worship and entertainment, schools, imposing residences and business premises (including the Markets); streets were widened, St. Peter Port and St. Sampson's harbours were greatly enlarged, roads were improved and communications by land and sea became something like they are today. This development continued into the Edwardian period, resulting in a pleasing emergence from a sometimes squalid (though often historic) settlement, without destroying the special charm still retained by St. Peter Port.

Happily, we can appreciate the island scene before the days of photography, thanks to numerous lithographs of the Bailiwick, especially those published by Matthew Moss in the 1830s. They were well drawn, tolerably accurate and certainly captured the atmosphere of the scenes depicted. Such 'old prints' are rightly treasured today and the reproductions available emphasise their popularity among islanders and visitors alike.

Photography reached the Guernsey Bailiwick in the 1850s and one of its pioneers was Carl Norman. *Barbet's Almanack* for 1858 contains an advertisement by J. B. Stonelake, of '8, New Road, Canichers' (Bruce Lane), offering Ambrotype, Daguerrotype and other portraits. By 1865, 13 photographic artists were listed. In *Rambles among the Channel Islands*, by 'A Naturalist', published in the 1850s, appears the following: 'Upon the shore of Fermain bay we made our first out-of-door photographic experiment', which the author described, mentioning that the use of a tent 'formed an exhaustless theme of wonder to some of the islanders'.

In the second edition of Ansted & Latham's *The Channel Islands*, published in 1865, the celebrated Guernsey artist Paul Naftel drew some of the illustrations of Guernsey and Sark from the photographs of a Dr. Mansell. Some excellent early photographs were taken of the enlargement of St. Peter Port harbour in the middle of the last century. However, despite the increasing popularity of the camera, photographs were rarely used to illustrate Victorian publications and never appeared in local newspapers of that era.

By the 1870s one could purchase excellent albums and photographic prints of places of interest in the Bailiwick. Notable was the work of Thomas Singleton, who sold wholeplate daylight-printed sepia views of town and harbour, shipping, buildings of historical significance and exquisite studies of Sark. His son, too, continued with the good work. However, these scenes rarely appeared in post-card form.

Early in the present century came the extremely numerous post-cards by Levy Brothers of Paris, whose cameras captured the island scene most successfully. Their cards sold at a halfpenny apiece and were also obtainable in packets and in tear-off booklet form. They were printed in France in both sepia and black and white (later issues were coloured) and, covering the Islands with the exception of Alderney, were of great value and charm. So were the artistic sepia reproductions of old Guernsey pictures, the work of F. W. Guerin. They included lithographs and early photographs.

The Alderney picture at the turn of the century was recorded by Thomas Westness, who was kept busy photographing wrecks, island life and interesting town and coastal scenes, mainly for tourists' benefit. Half-plate views were sold at 6d. each and post-cards at 2d. apiece. Westness first worked in Guernsey from 1884 until about 1900; he moved to Alderney, remaining there until 1919, when he retired to Guernsey again.

Coloured photographic cards proved most successful when they appeared some seventy years ago. Indeed, their good looks put most modern post-cards to shame! Many of the coloured and black and white cards were published by such firms as Valentine, Photochrom and Tuck.

Pre-war Guernsey was much photographed by Thomas Bramley, who specialised in local happenings of importance, although much of his work was devoted to studies of town and harbour. He frequently visited the other Islands and his pictures are prized today. His contemporary, Norman Grut, was chiefly engaged in studio work, though his father, Thomas, was probably more versatile and took many landscapes. T. B. Banks & Company were also responsible for some interesting Guernsey illustrations. Of this period, J. A. Hamson was a noted studio photographer.

Charles Toms (1887–1957) served the Guernsey Press Co. Ltd. for over forty years and his camera studies were outstanding. Photography was his hobby as well as his work, and the results were as meticulous as they were excellent in composition and artistry. He was an Associate of the Royal Photographic Society and president of the Guernsey Photographic Society. Retiring to Sark, he continued his work, delighting in reproducing 19th-century photographs as much as in contemporary studies.

The light enjoyed in the Guernsey Bailiwick, together with the wealth of pictorial material appeal it offers, have made local photography something of major importance for over a century. It has placed on record scenes of historical and personal interest; and it has preserved pictorially many an object, whether building, locality or prospect, which, but for the camera, might have been lost to posterity. For a good deal of this the island camera clubs and many other individual photographers warrant our thanks.

The pains taken by pioneers in this art-form were remarkable, and resulted in capital pictures we now enjoy. Happily, great numbers of them have been preserved, though this book can include but a fraction of the material available. Some of the photographs have come from private collections, others from the Priaulx and Guille-Allès Libraries and they clearly form a contribution of some merit to the Bailiwick's history.

I

SHIPS AND HARBOURS

In the mid-19th century, when St. Peter Port harbour was undergoing massive enlargement, many doubtless believed its size was out of all proportion to its needs. Perhaps that was true at the time, but those responsible for the development were men of vision, foreseeing the need of a port far bigger than the diminutive and wholly tidal Old Harbour which was quite inadequate.

The planners were right and today we have reason to thank them, even though the New Harbour had to be developed further when the Jetty was built. Nevertheless, in the last century, what was once the Inner Road was incorporated within the harbour arms, Castle Cornet was united with St. Peter Port and the environs of the resultant spacious haven were also developed most satisfactorily.

In 1862 the London & South Western Railway Company was authorised to own and operate ships; it accordingly assumed control of the New South Western Steam Navigation Company and began a service between Southampton and the Channel Islands which continued until 1961. The Weymouth packet service was much older.

The first Southampton ships of the period were the paddlers *Normandy* and *Brittany*, each of about six hundred gross tons. Another was the *St. Malo,* of rather similar tonnage, but a screw steamer with a much more modern profile. In 1867 came the first *Caesarea*, a smaller vessel, and a year later the *Waverley* arrived, propelled by paddles. She was wrecked in 1873 on the Platte Boue rock off Guernsey, but without loss of life.

The mail destined for Jersey was taken there by HMS *Dasher*, a fishery protection ship and formerly a Weymouth mail packet. A paddler of 250 tons, she was completed in 1838 and carried passengers and mail for seven years before being used for other purposes. When she returned to island waters she was a familiar sight until, in 1884, she was replaced by a former gunboat, HMS *Mistletoe*.

The *Havre*, another Southampton paddle steamer, also came to grief on the Platte Boue. This was in 1875 and, like the *Waverley*, she was completely lost, though there were no casualties. In the previous year the screw steamer *Guernsey* arrived in island ports. Of 572 tons, she was wrecked off Cap de la Hague in 1915. A contemporary was the *Honfleur*, of 429 tons, which ran between Jersey and Granville, but sometimes used St. Peter Port. She was still afloat in 1969 and was then 96 years old!

Several Southampton mail ships resembled each other, notably the *Diana*, *Ella*, *Laura*, *Dora* and *Hilda*, the last of which was wrecked off St. Malo in 1905 with the loss of 128 lives. These attractive little steamers were succeeded by the even finer *Frederica*, *Lydia* and *Stella*. In 1899 the *Stella* struck the Casquets off Alderney and foundered, taking with her 105 lives. A stewardess, Mrs. Mary Rogers, gave her life-jacket to a passenger and was drowned.

For Many years the Weymouth link had been maintained by the Weymouth & Channel Islands Steam Packet Company, but in 1889 this was purchased by the Great Western Railway, whose fast and handsome *Lynx*, *Gazelle* and *Antelope* are still recalled by aged islanders. Their speed was 18 knots, they were of 609 tons and the *Lynx* and *Gazelle* were later converted into cargo vessels, remaining in service until 1925. The *Antelope* was sold in 1913. With their two red funnels and graceful lines, these little packets were much admired, even though they were lively in rough weather.

In 1891 the *Ibex* joined the Weymouth fleet and ran on the service for many years, including the Great War period. In 1900 she struck a rock near the Platte Fougère and sank with the loss of two lives. She was later raised, repaired at St. Sampson's and towed to England for further attention. She was broken up in 1926.

Similar were the *Reindeer* and *Roebuck*. The former was first seen here in 1897 and left us in 1926. The latter was sunk in collision with a battleship in 1915. Contemporaries and rivals of these vessels were the LSWR *Vera* of 1898 and the *Alberta* of 1900, a ship which replaced the *Stella*. The former survived until 1933, but the latter was afloat as late as 1941, when she was sunk on war service.

Finally, the period under review saw the *Sarnia* and *Caesarea*, fine Southampton boats, built in 1910 and of over 1500 tons. The *Sarnia* was lost in the war of 1914, but her sister survived until 1950. Like all LSWR ships, they had buff funnels, contrasting with the scarlet of the GWR.

As well as mail steamers, the railway companies had cargo vessels. From Southampton came the *Ada*, *Bertha* and *Brittany* (later renamed *Aldershot*), as well as occasional sailings by the *Cherbourg*. Additional to the *Lynx* and *Gazelle*, the Weymouth cargo fleet included the *Pembroke*. Most of these had accommodation for 12 passengers.

Perhaps the best-loved island ship of all was the *Courier*, a graceful steamer of 151 tons, which operated with her predecessor, the 'Little' *Courier*, on the Guernsey-Alderney service for a great many years. Occasionally she sailed to Cherbourg and ran excursions to Sark, like the *Alert*, *Serk* and *Assistance*, of the Guernsey Steam Towing & Trading Company. These were also tugs, often used for towing sailing craft in and out of port and occasionally employed on salvage work. All these vessels were familiar sights at St. Peter Port at the turn of the century and later.

The little *Fawn* plied regularly between Guernsey, St. Malo and Poole (replacing a sailing cutter of the same name) and running to Sark towards the end of the last century was the paddle steamer *Rescue*, which succeeded a craft of a similar name. The sailing boat *Mermaid* ran across to Herm (then a private island) and sailing cutters went to Sark as well as steamers. The cutters' fares were lower than their rivals, but passengers were expected to help with the rowing if the wind failed!

Regular cargo services linked Guernsey with England. Steamers came from London (they included the *Island Queen, London Queen* and *Ocean Queen*), carrying a few passengers as well as freight. There were shipping links with other ports, including Bristol, Plymouth and French harbours. One of the best-known Plymouth ships was the *Channel Queen*, rather resembling the *Lynx*. She was lost off Portinfer in 1898, and a memorial to those who perished stands in St. Sampson's churchyard.

In the Old Harbour berthed sailing ships bringing coal to the island. In the Albert Dock (now a marina) timber was discharged and temporarily stacked on what is now the bus terminus. Sometimes vessels unloaded live cattle for slaughter virtually at the doors of the abbatoir. On the careening hard was a patent slip, on mobile cradles, often occupied by vessels needing painting or repairs.

The life-boat was moored in the Pool, off the Castle emplacement, where the Royal National Life-boat Institution's shed was sited. It stood beside the Model Yacht Pond, opened in 1887 as a memorial to Queen Victoria's Golden Jubilee. Our earlier life-boats were based at St. Sampson's, but in 1862 the *Louisa Hall* was moved to St. Peter Port, which became the home of her successors, the *John Lockett, Vincent Wilkinson Kirkella* and the last of the pulling and sailing boats, the *Arthur Lionel*, dating from 1912.

If the life-boat was needed off the west coast, it was customary to take her across the island on a mobile cradle drawn by a team of horses. Although wrecks were frequent in the last century, more often than not local ships went to the rescue because of their superior power and speed. Sometimes the steam pilot cutter *Vixen* rendered aid or, later, the motor pilot boat *Stork*, both of which were moored in the Pool.

In this spacious area of St. Peter Port stately yachts anchored. Some were steamers, others spread an elegant area of sail. If they were very large they dropped anchor in the roadstead, where big warships were sometimes seen. The Pool and the roads were also used by windbound sailers, vessels sheltering and others awaiting berths or a favourable tide. Off St. Peter Port the War Department steamer *Sir Redvers Bulwer* was occasionally seen towing targets at which the guns of Castle Cornet or Clarence battery fired.

At St. Sampson's more colliers discharged and, until about 1900, the vast majority were sailing craft. Some were of the fleet of Onesimus Dorey, who later introduced an impressive number of steamers, all registered in

Guernsey. These coal boats normally returned to England laden with granite, which had been crushed at quayside mills, having been quarried near this northern port.

St. Sampson's also had a careening hard, where ships were hauled up for attention. On the South Side was the yard of Peter Ogier, where many fine sailing vessels were built in the last century. By no means all of these were in local employment, since most sailed the Seven Seas. Here they were also repaired and sometimes lengthened. Other shipyards were on beaches flanking the North and South Esplanades, the Piette and Hougue à la Perre. Shipbuilding was an important island industry between 1815 and 1895 and the construction of small craft remains significant.

Around Guernsey's shores are several attractive fishing havens, though today, when craft under sail are no more, they are less picturesque than they were a century ago. The harbours remain in use by fishermen, divers and anglers. They are at La Salerie, La Tonnelle, Bordeaux, Les Ammareurs, Rousse, Portelet and La Moye, with smaller piers between them. At St. Peter Port, St. Sampson's, Grand Havre and Rocquaine, regattas were held in the past and those of St. Sampson's and Rocquaine have been revived. Formerly, the Sark regatta was extremely popular.

Les Hanois light shone for the first time in 1862 and thereafter shipwrecks around the Guernsey coast decreased somewhat, though they still remained fairly numerous. When lighthouses were built on La Platte Fougère in 1909, Alderney in 1912 and Sark in 1913, numbers dropped more appreciably.

Between 1860 and 1914 over a hundred wrecks occurred around Guernsey alone. Not all of them resulted in total loss, naturally, but several were serious. About forty vessels were wrecked around Alderney during that period. Many photographs were taken of the stranded *Ocean Queen* off Les Tielles in 1906 and of the celebrated wreck of the *Liverpool* at Alderney in 1902.

Another noteworthy calamity also occurred in Alderney waters: the loss of the destroyer *Viper* during the 1901 manoeuvres. More photographs were taken of the *Leros, Petit Raymond* and *Felix de Abasolo*, stranded off Alderney early in the present century, among other vessels. Three more, in Guernsey waters, also claimed the photographers' attention: the brigantine *Dunsinane* (1904), the *Courier* and the *Swansea* (both in 1906). With the introduction of radio and the increase in lighthouses and other navigational aids, shipwrecks declined in numbers as the 20th century waxed older.

1. This 1854 photograph shows the old 17 ft wide Quay extending along the inner face of the Old Harbour, which was built between 1775 and 1779. The tunnel of La Rue des Vaches can be seen by the gantry on the left, which shows the starting of work on the New Harbour, whose foundation stone was laid in 1853.

2. The foundation stone of the New Harbour of St. Peter Port was laid on 24 August 1853, near where this picture was taken several months later, on 31 March 1854. Trucks ran along a gantry, below which the Castle Pier was built.

3. The south arm of the Old Harbour nearing completion in 1861, after its rebuilding. The lighthouse and lock-up for prisoners awaiting transport by sea to Castle Cornet were built in 1832. A wooden construction replaces the structure, which was far more graceful than its successor.

4. In 1865, the date of this photograph, the Castle lighthouse was still not built, though the breakwater was almost completed. Neither was there a lighthouse at the White Rock, although the actual rock of that name had been built over. St. Julian's pier, leading to the White Rock, and the adjoining emplacement, are visible on the left.

5. St. Peter Port harbour in 1866, showing passengers disembarking from what was probably a vessel from Weymouth, a paddle steamer just visible at the extremity of the breakwater. This was used for a temporary landing place. On 3 March 1867 the lighthouse there was lit for the first time.

6. The old North Pier, St. Peter Port, in 1882. Now called the Victoria Pier, it was virtually rebuilt late in the last century and its ancient appearance disappeared. The photograph shows several sailing vessels berthed there, with the Crown Hotel and other buildings in the background. Trees mark the site of the States Office.

7. St. Peter Port quayside in about 1900. An electric tram and a couple of horse-drawn vehicles comprise the traffic along a road which today teems with it. Sailing ships with coal line the quays; opposite them are cellars, stores and marine warehouses, as well as pubs, hotels and, rising above them, the Town Church spire.

8. The barque *Courier* on the careening hard, St. Peter Port, in August 1873. The first slip was built at a cost of £2,804 and was completed on 12 April 1872. In November 1873 the States decided to build a second slip.

9.   The Albert Dock area of St. Peter Port seen from the 'broken wall', with the steamer *Alert* alongside the Albert Pier. Much of this part of the harbour is now a yacht marina.

10.   The steamer *Alert* at Creux Harbour, Sark, early in the present century. Owned by the Guernsey Steam Towing & Trading Company, she was employed on excursion work and occasional towing. Similar was the *Serk*, and both bore a superficial resemblance to the *Courier*.

11. The Southampton mail steamer *Stella* at St. Peter Port in 1897. Two years later she struck the Casquets reef, west of Alderney, and foundered, taking with her 105 lives. A stewardess, Mrs. Mary Rogers, gave her life-jacket to a passenger and was drowned.

12. The steamer *Assistance* leaving St. Peter Port in about 1900. She was owned by the Guernsey Steam Towing Trading Company and was used for towing and excusions to Sark and Herm.

13. The paddle steamer *Rescue I* about to leave the Albert Dock. She was used for harbour work, towing and excursions, and was succeeded by another paddler, *Rescue II,* in 1878. The extremity of the Albert Pier (right) bears small resemblance to its present appearance.

14. The paddle steamer *Rescue II* anchored off Les Laches, Sark, in 1878. When Creux Harbour dried out, ships were obliged to anchor outside, when passengers were landed by Sark fishing boats.

15. (*left*) In 1894 the ketch *Sarnia*, built at Ogier's yard, St. Sampson's, was launched. She was the last cargo and passenger vessel of her kind to be built there. A *Star* correspondent, Thomas Toms, wrote: '. . . Captain Samuel Gillman gave orders to slip the buoy ropes and, like a thing of life, the *Sarnia* leapt forth and at the first start proved herself able to sail close to the wind, for she went clear out without tacking'.

16. (*below*) H.M.S. *Mistletoe*, a fishery protection vessel, at St. Peter Port in July 1884. These ships were based in the Channel Islands, principally to protect the valuable Jersey oyster fishery and to keep a watchful eye on possible smugglers. The *Mistletoe* was originally a gunboat.

17. The Plymouth steamer *Channel Queen* was wrecked off Port Soif, Guernsey, in 1898. She was locally-owned and rather resembled the Great Western Railway's *Lynx*.

18. (*left*) The brigantine *Dunsinane*, hard ashore off St. Sampson's harbour on 13 August 1904. She struck the Black Rock, a hazard near the entrance.

19. The wreck of the s.s. *Rhenania* on the islet of Burhou on 8 April 1912. Just visible alongside is the Guernsey salvage steamer *Pioneer*, letting off steam.

Wreck on Burhou—S.S. "Rhenania," April 8th, 1912

20. The life-boat *John Lockett* in 1875. She was first based at La Lande Point, Vale. In this photograph she is seen outside her station at the North Side, Vale.

21. The Platte Fougère lighthouse under construction in 1909. A mile and a half off the north-east corner of the island, it cost about £10,000 and was hailed as a great achievement. The octagonal tower was built of concrete and became the first lighthouse in the British Isles to be unattended and controlled from the shore by means of a submarine cable. Before the lighthouse was built a wooden beacon stood on the rock bearing the letters PF. The letter P can be seen above the structure. The steamer is the 47-ton *Pioneer*, used for carrying supplies to the rock.

22. (*above*) The steamer *Swansea* of Swansea, ashore at Vazon on 23 July 1906. She struck the notorious North West Grunes and was beached on the sands, where her cargo of coal was removed in box-carts. After some days, during which crowds visited the scene, she was refloated.

23. (*left*) A Guernsey fishing boat at anchor. Craft like this were built in the island, and until recently there were a few survivors. They spread a large sail area in proportion to their size and consisted of two types: mackerel drifters and crabbers. This craft was a drifter.

24. (*right*) Fishing craft taking part in the Grand Havre regatta in 1908. Left centre is a mackerel drifter under sail.

25. A scene at the White Rock in the early 1890s. The elegant Great Western Railway's booking office, refreshment rooms and stores were built in 1892 and have since been demolished; the stone was used to build lavatories elsewhere. These were the days when wicker baskets were used to export tomatoes, horses and carts were the only means of transport, and steam cranes were employed to load and unload ships.

26. The granite port of St. Sampson in about 1870, from where thousands of tons of stone were exported to Britain. The photograph was taken from Mont Crevelt.

27.   An animated scene at the White Rock in about 1910. Tomatoes and flowers are being loaded onto the wait-
ing Southampton steamer and passengers wait to board the ship. Horses and vans stand unattended and there is a
general air of seeming chaos before sailing time.

II

FORTIFICATIONS

When photographers became really active in the Guernsey Bailiwick they seldom viewed its fortifications through their lenses, and this is a pity, since such pictures would be invaluable today. Probably photographers and artists would have been debarred from taking pictures within the defences, and possibly they were even discouraged from so doing outside them. Thus, only distant views are for the most part now available.

Guernsey and Alderney bristled with active fortifications a century ago, even though there had been no warfare since 1815. Yet the French were still suspect and the Cherbourg defences of the 1840s prompted the British Government to fortify Alderney anew and, in some measure, to improve defences in the other Islands. Alderney's breakwater and forts were complementary to Brèhon tower, in the Little Russel, and there were improvements effected at Castle Cornet and Fort George.

The garrison was retained and a large Militia helped to man the numerous guns, which were not removed until the end of the last century. Guernsey's principal stronghold was Fort George, though the general public was at liberty to go there, provided the citadel and gun positions were avoided. Castle Cornet could be visited only with a pass, but the coastal forts were of lesser importance, although troops were sometimes stationed at Fort Houmet. Many batteries still retained their guns and several were used for Militia training. Local troops also practised with the cannon at Castle Cornet and Clarence battery.

Arsenals were built in several parishes, serving as Militia headquarters, prior to the building of Beaucamps camp in 1901. At the arsenals, bands practised, troops drilled and instruction was received. Here were housed arms, ammunition and equipment. Large-scale parades and sham-fights were frequent and these were usually watched by the Lieutenant-Governor, who commanded the island's armed forces. The artillery horses were the property of the War Department, but were cared for by farmers when not on active service.

Outlying forts were linked with Fort George by military roads, the inspiration of Lieut.-Gen. Sir John Doyle, Guernsey's most brilliant Lieutenant-Governor, who held office from 1803 to 1816. He was also instrumental in the reclamation of the Braye du Valle (a channel of water separating the Clos du Valle from the rest of the island), thus making possible the rapid movement of troops from Fort George to the north of the island.

Small wonder that one of the Vale forts was named after Doyle and that a column to his memory was raised at Jerbourg. It was destroyed during the German Occupation, like the stately obelisk in Delancey Park, erected to the memory of Admiral Lord de Saumarez. During the Napoleonic wars he commanded the naval squadron based on Guernsey's roadstead. A west coast fort is named after him.

Additional to the forts and coastal batteries were the watch-houses, some of which survive. From these lonely outposts the Militia were on the look-out for the French, often for months on end. Elaborate precautions were taken to prevent landings, and equally complex plans were made to rout the foe if he set foot ashore. Playing a part in these measures were the Martello towers, today so much of the seaboard picture. The watch-houses had a signalling system and long-distance messages were also exchanged with Telegraph Tower, Alderney, and the signal post at Le Mât, Sark.

In the latter half of the last century, when it was appreciated that the French had no evil designs on the Islands, precautions were relaxed, most of the forts and batteries passing into the hands of the States and ultimately becoming the ancient monuments they are today. Their artillery was removed, and by the end of the 19th century only Fort George and Castle Cornet were garrisoned. Of these, the fort was by far the more important.

Fort Doyle became valuable again for another reason. In 1909 a light-house was built on La Platte Fougère rock and the fort was used as an alternative fog signal station and lighthouse store. Nearby the telegraph cable came ashore from England, so that this north-eastern corner of Guernsey was still of strategic importance. The same might be said of St. Martin's point, where the cable left Guernsey for Jersey and where another lighthouse has been erected.

Even with the decline of its military importance, Guernsey, like Alderney, presented a colourful picture up to 1914. The garrison soldiers in their scarlet and blue, the Militia in similar uniform, the strains of bugle calls and martial music, the presence of troops on and off duty, all produced a lively, bracing atmosphere, and the social and sporting aspects of island life bene-fited accordingly. The outbreak of war in 1914 did not rob the islands of their military significance, but the picture changed from one of gaiety to a far more sombre scene.

28. (left) The Pleinmont guardhouse, which stood on the Torteval cliffs, as it looked in 1910. It became known as 'The Haunted House' because Victor Hugo called it thus in his novel, *The Toilers of the Sea*. This he wrote while exiled in Guernsey. The building was given a flat roof during the First World War, when it was used as a signalling station, but during the German Occupation it was destroyed.

29. (below) Legend has it that the moated Château des Marais, originally known as Le Château d'Orgueil, was built in the 11th century on the orders of Robert, Duke of Normandy, in gratitude for the hospitality he received when in Guernsey. There is no documentary evidence to support this, however. For a period it was the residence of the Governors of Guernsey. Within its walls was La Chapelle de Notre Dame des Marais, a royal chapel. In the 18th century the defences were strengthened to combat the threat of possible French invasion.

30. (*above*) The Royal Guernsey Militia
Artillery band. It was photographed at
L'Ancresse Common, probably during an
exercise, in about 1880.

31. (*right*) Royal Guernsey Militia
Infantrymen, in the uniform of a century
ago.

32. A King's Birthday parade at Belvedere Field, Fort George, photographed in about 1912.
resident troops and members of the Royal Guernsey Militia. Hundreds of men are seen marc
spectacle was attended by thousands of spectators and was one of the highlights of the Guer

an annual event until 1939, when the garrison was withdrawn. Taking part were the Fort's the Lieutenant-Governor, with the massed bands in the centre of the parade. This magnificent ndar.

33. The band of the 1st Regiment, Royal Guernsey Militia, photographed towards the close of the 19th century. The prominent figure on the right is Drum-Major W.H. Courtenay. The picture was taken at Cambridge Park, where the Town Regiment paraded.

34. A Guernsey Rifle Association meeting at L'Ancresse. Members comprise Militiamen and civilians, as well as a lady and an elderly man in a top hat, possibly non-members.

35. A group of bandsmen of the 2nd Battalion, the Manchester Regiment, who were stationed at Fort George in 1904.

III

INDUSTRY AND TRANSPORT

In the past, Guernsey was much more self-sufficient than it is today. While many commodities were imported, much was manufactured locally: far more than is now the case. Reference has already been made to ship-building (which also embraced such subsidiary industries as rope-making, sail-making and metal-working), to the export of stone and, of course, to agriculture and horticulture.

Fishing is important and was so in the last century, though on a different scale, when craft were propelled by sails and, sometimes, oars. Fishermen used large mackerel boats when working far out to sea and the smaller crabbers for inshore catches. They made their own nets, crab pots and 'courges' (in which sand-eel bait was kept alive) and did as much maintenance work as possible. In many instances they were part-time fishermen, often working on the land as well. To some extent, this is still the case.

Despite the fact that so many island buildings are of stone, bricks were manufactured here in great quantities. There were brickfields at St. Andrew's, St. Martin's, St. Peter Port and at Oatlands, L'Islet; in the last instance the kilns are still standing. Soap was manufactured in Le Truchot, St. Peter Port, and there were iron foundries at La Hougue à la Perre and elsewhere. Gas was first made in Guernsey in 1830.

Tinsmiths were busy in St. Peter Port, making among other objects Guernsey cans, used in the dairy industry and domestically. They were of tin, although the ornamental ones were of brass or copper. Happily, cans are still made locally. Incidentally, the dairy products included butter (made on the farms and bearing their imprints), curds and cream. Butter was often sold in the market on cabbage leaves.

Then, as now, beer was brewed in the island, and there were numerous mineral-water manufactories in the town. Allied to the brewing trade was the making of casks by coopers, who also made barrels for other purposes. On a different note, mention should be made of the manufacture of iodine from seaweed. There was a small factory on Lihou island and, also on the west coast, seaweed was burnt on the beach for the extraction of its potash content. The so-called 'Roman cement' was made at Les Vardes. A chicory factory was in the Steam Mill Lanes, St. Martin's.

In the past much clothing and footwear were made locally, and these industries must have been in competition with imported goods of this nature. An almanack of a century ago listed 31 bakers, 15 cabinet makers and six umbrella makers. There were also people who made dressed dolls out of fish shells, as well as the doll known as 'Cobo Alice', because it was first made in that region. Tobacco was manufactured in Guernsey (in a small way it still is) and wine matured in great vaults in St. Peter Port. Guernsey 'sugars' were made until quite recently, and these sweets are greatly missed today.

Turning to the subject of transport, islanders in the last century and early in the present one were usually more inclined to walk than to ride. For one thing it was cheaper, and for another there was sometimes no alternative unless, of course, one was wealthy. For the well-to-do there were horses and carriages, but for the rank and file there were few, if any, means of public transport. It is true that a horse bus service operated between St. Peter Port and St. Sampson's from as early as 1837, but this was an exception.

All kinds of conveyances were made in the island, whether they were elegant carriages for the gentry or box-carts for the farmer. The farmer also used long carts (similar vehicles, but open at either end) and sledges, as well as wheelbarrows and, naturally, ploughs, all of which were Guernsey-made. When horse bus services became more numerous, these big vehicles were also of local manufacture. They operated between town and St. Martin's, Cobo and occasionally went to the Forest and further west.

Horse buses also plied along the east coast in competition with the trams. Steam cars were first introduced in 1879 and were succeeded by electric trams in 1892. The Guernsey Railway Company operated them and was the first to introduce motor buses in about 1909. They ran from Les Banques to L'Islet and from St. Sampson's to L'Ancresse, operating in conjunction with the trams.

The electric cars were double-deckers and on busy days trailers were attached, of the 'toastrack' variety. The cars stopped anywhere on request, and sometimes the service would be halted because of heavy seas hurling stones on the line. The tram service ceased in 1934, by which time horse buses had given way to motor vehicles. However, four-horsed wagonettes (again in 'toastrack' fashion) still conveyed tourists around the island until after that year.

Livery stables were numerous in the past. They supplied landaus and the more humble 'chairs', as well as hearses and wedding coaches. One could also hire smaller vehicles like dogcarts or governess cars and drive them personally. There were ranks for cabs in the town and at the harbour, as there are for taxis nowadays.

Bicycles became very popular, first appearing in 'penny farthing' form. They were used as sporting machines, and the Cycling Track at Victoria Avenue was originally designed for bicycle races. In time, machines became cheaper and even more were seen on the roads. Island thoroughfares used to be rough going, however, since their surfaces were mainly intended for the use of horses. Today, the bicycle is chiefly used by visitors who hire them, as they do motor cars—vehicles first seen in the island at the turn of the century.

36.   Petit Bôt in about 1900. Three buildings are of interest. The Martello tower was built in about 1778 and cost £100. Behind are two water mills. There had been one mill—probably a wooden building—in this area before 1248. In 1701 the upper mill and an adjoining house were constructed, and in about 1752 the lower mill came into being. Both were used to grind corn, but in 1827 the lower mill, now tearooms, was converted for the manufacture of paper from rags. A Guernsey newspaper, *L'Indépendence*, of 29 February 1829, was printed on paper made there. Both mills ceased to function in the 1850s.

37.   One of Le Couteur's mackerel boats at Rocquaine in about 1880. A little earlier there were some 24 Guernsey drifters such as these operating off the south coast of England.

38. Quarry workings at Les Romains, L'Islet, in about 1910. Granite has been extracted for local building and for export since about 1794. In 1913 exports to Britain reached a peak of 500,000 tons. At one time there were as many as 268 quarries being worked in Guernsey.

39. Anthracite coal was imported from South Wales by the thousands of tons for heating glasshouses growing grapes and tomatoes. This photograph was taken at the Old Harbour early in 1914.

40.   Rope-makers at work at St. John's rope walk in about 1899. On 'A Plan of the Town of St. Peter's Port and Environs, 1843' is marked 'Le Tissier's Rope Walk'. In 1865 the contracts of the property, where a small building was used for boiling tar, described it as 'une corderie', with 'mecaniques', or pieces of machinery. A row of trees grew along the full length of the south side of the walk to provide shade for the moistened strands of rope.

41 & 42. R. J. Collins' Guernsey sweet factory in about 1880. Robert James Collins started making 'sugars' in 1879 and the firm finally closed down in 1975. The second photograph shows sugar being delivered to the works.

43. (*left*) A typical town shop in the early part of the present century. The proprietors, Mr. and Mrs. George Williams, stand at the door of their grocery business in Lower Vauvert in about 1903, together with their son and dog. Although the shopfront has changed, the balcony above it survives

44. (*below*) St. Peter Port Market Place in about 1880. A few 'open air' stall-holders are still using the traditional site, though the majority have moved their stalls to the spacious buildings nearby. The cobblestones of the Square unfortunately belong to the past, and today the place is a car park.

45. F. B. Guerin's mobile book and postcard stand which had to be wheeled from High Street to its pitch at the White Rock to meet the mailboat from England or Jersey.

46. A linotype operator at the Guernsey Press Co. Ltd. in 1913. This machine was first used in Britain in 1890. The company installed its first type-setting machine in 1902. The operator is Mr. Charles H. Toms.

TRANSPORT ILLUSTRATIONS

47. Today, St. Peter Port's bus terminus scarcely resembles the tram terminus of yesterday. Two cars are outside the Picquet House, while by the People's Café is a double-decked horse bus. It ran to St. Sampson's, like the trams. The trees mark the site of the present bus station.

48. The first steam tram car to operate between St. Peter Port and St. Sampson's. It started the service on 6 June 1879; trams later driven by electricity, remained until 9 June 1934.

49. (*left*) Tramcar No.1 at St. Sampson's Bridge early in the present century. It is seen leaving the terminus; another tram is visible on the right. A box-cart and a governess car are on the left.

50. (*below right*) A four-in-hand excursion car out in the country. From its high perches an excellent view could be had, and to sit beside the driver was deemed a privilege. Cars like this survived in Guernsey until the 1930s.

51. (*below left*) The St. Martin's bus at Le Petit Carrefour, or 'Top of the Market', in 1902. In winter the vehicle was closed in; otherwise it was open to the elements, and in wet weather umbrellas were sometimes used by passengers.

52. Horse-drawn wagonettes (fours-in-hand) were the form of transport chosen by parties wishing to travel the countryside or go to the beach for a picnic. They were also popular among visitors touring the island. This is a staff outing of Sydney Frampton, coachbuilder, of 29 Victoria Road, St. Peter Port, in about 1900. At this period there were some 18 coach and carriage builders in Guernsey, including Frederick Coysh, grandfather of the co-author, whose Paragon Works were in Park Street.

53. One of the island's first motor buses operated by the Guernsey Railway Co. Ltd. was this 1912 conversion from a landau. The driver is a Mr. Baker. The bus was photographed at L'Islet cross-roads.

IV

HORTICULTURE

Victorian topographical works were often loud in their praise of the gardens of Guernsey. In those spacious days the landed gentry, in their fine residences, could afford to keep large staffs, and gardeners maintained their grounds in splendid order. Some of the most noted were those of Saumarez Park, its neighbours St. George and La Haye du Puits, and Sausmarez Manor. Nearer the town were Mon Plaisir (with its great fig tree), Montville (the house is no more), Beau Sejour (whose grounds are sports areas) and Valnord.

Candie Gardens, before they became public property, were very productive. Mention should be made of the grounds of La Seigneurie, Sark, Herm's gardens beside the mansion, the ancient mulberry tree at Jethou and the specious property surrounding what is now the Island Hall, Alderney.

The books stressed the excellence of our pears, apples, peaches and figs, grown in walled gardens of some size, and of more exotic fruits raised in hothouses, including melons. The island gardens were (and still are) beautified by stately trees and by such ornamental shrubs as camellia, hydrangea, rhododendron and magnolia. Many of them may well have been reared at the Caledonia Nursery. Among the flowers were arums and the lovely Guernsey lily. Ferns were also noteworthy.

In 1863, Charles Smith of the Caledonia Nursery was the first to send flowers to the London market. They were camellias. A year later the first consignment of spring flowers was despatched to London. Before the days of steamers such exports would have been impossible, at least commercially.

Bulbs were originally grown in gardens as clumps. Gradually their export became of importance, and as much as 450 tons were sent away annually. Outdoor spring flowers were grown for export, including daffodils, narcissi, gladioli, anemones, arums, irises and tulips. By 1905 over 450,000 packages were exported annually. When the First World War broke out in 1914 these numbers were reduced.

The decline of Guernsey ship-building roughly coincided with the birth of what is now our major industry: horticulture. Thus, the men who built the sailing vessels found employment in glasshouse construction. In these structures excellent grapes were grown and, exported in trays, were in great demand in London and elsewhere. The greenhouse properties became known as vineries, and the name has been transferred to the tomato houses of today.

The tomato rapidly proved to be more profitable than the grape (although choice black and white fruit continued to be grown and, in a very small way, is still cultivated in Guernsey) and by 1874 the so-called 'Love Apple' had bloomed into a thriving industry. The historian F. B. Tupper noted that in that year a local company was formed to export tomatoes to London and other markets. The vineries were 'on the sunny slope of Delancey Hill', St. Sampson's, and covered an acre and a half.

Prominent Victorian and Edwardian growers included Messrs. S. J. Falla, Hubert & Mauger, E. H. Wheadon and Peter Ozanne. Their produce travelled to St. Peter Port in horse-drawn vans, laden with wicker baskets which were returnable. In the early days produce travelled by mail steamer and fast train to the markets. Later, special cargo vessels took the fruit and flowers to England.

Much of the island produce was, of course, on sale locally, and it is still a tourist attraction to see the glorious array of flowers in our markets. Equally impressive are the fruit and vegetables there, particularly in the French Halles. About a century ago a new vegetable market was built, facing the Town Church, and today this is chiefly devoted to flowers.

Guernsey has several nurseries where trees and plants thrive in attractive surroundings. Many private gardens which won Victorian acclaim are now open to the public, at stated times, in aid of charities. Their appeal is as strong as ever. Likewise, the properties of the National Trust of Guernsey are available for public enjoyment, and the wild flowers blooming there add a colourful touch to the glory of the scene.

54. The island's earliest glasshouses were built by private owners to give shelter for fruit, but islanders quickly realised the potential of the grape and miles of glasshouses were constructed. As early as 1830 some 3,474 lbs. of grapes were exported. The work entailed in thinning the fruit was tremendous, and women using specially pointed scissors were employed for this task. To reach the bunches they had to sit on movable steps and it was a task which required much patience. The vinery was also a place where women could gossip as they worked.

55. A glasshouse of poinsettias and smilax being tended by the Misses Henrietta and Unice Ogier, at Duveaux Farm, St. Sampson's, in about 1902.

56. Picking grapes in a vinery in about 1900. In 1855 scarcely three tons of
fruit were exported, but this figure rose rapidly and special grape cases were used
to transport the produce to the United Kingdom by sea. When grape growing
declined the vineries were used for tomato growing.

57.   Workers on a tomato vinery. Tomatoes were first grown in clay pots, many of which were made in the island. Anthracite for heating the glasshouses was imported from South Wales. On the left is a stoker with his shovel. Other workers are seen with tomato plants, grapes and baskets of tomatoes. Behind is the carter who travelled with his horse and van to and from the vinery to the White Rock, St. Peter Port.

58.   A typical two-horse van used for the transport of 12 lb. wicker baskets of tomatoes to the steamer at the White Rock. The baskets were returned to growers after use. The van was also used for carting hay when equipped with spreading hay ladders at front and back. Another use for it was for taking the farmer and his family to town or to a picnic somewhere on the coast. During the German Occupation such vans were used as omnibuses.

V

AGRICULTURE

Archaeologists believe that island agriculture began when prehistoric man settled here. There were group settlements who, preferably on high ground and near a water supply, cultivated the land, working on a communal basis on the 'Open Field' system. Traces of this early strip farming survive in Alderney, at Les Camps, St. Martin's and elsewhere.

Very much later came the formation of parishes, the creation of fiefs, the building of churches and the gradual evolution of Guernsey as we know it today. Waste land was reclaimed and farming became an established industry, supplying islanders with food and drink. Orchards, too, were important, and the making of cider was widespread.

The gradual enclosure of land and the substantial hedges which resulted spelt the decline of open field farming, although the right of 'banan' (making arable land available for communal pasture following the harvest) was not abolished until 1717. When the introduction of parsnip growing became popular the need for deeper trenching resulted in the use of 'La Grande Querue' (the big plough), which was of local construction (like all vehicles and implements) and of an extraordinary size.

It was customary for the plough to be jointly owned by farmers living near each other, who supplied the beasts to draw it. Six horses and four oxen were usually employed, although smaller ploughs naturally needed fewer animals. Farmers also supplied the necessary labour, and these men were usually regaled with meat and drink at the end of the day, together with rural rejoicing. When the task was finished the plough was taken to another farm and, planting over, it was kept by one of the owners until it was needed again.

A great many of the existing farmhouses were built in the 18th century. A typical building would have a massive entrance arch, possibly with the initials of the husband and wife who built it carved on the keystone, with the date and perhaps a heart at either extremity. There might be four dormer windows on each of the two floors, and the thatched roof (later pantiled) would have stone chimney stacks at each end. Quite probably these would be provided with stone projections, which were sometimes believed to have been set there to provide resting places for witches, who otherwise might have entered the house! In fact, the stones served a far more practical purpose: to shed rain onto the thatch at a point where it met the chimney. At the rear of the house was the 'tourelle', or circular staircase. The building's walls were very thick, like the massive entrance arch at the roadside. This might well be a double one, with the larger arch for vehicles and the smaller for pedestrians.

Within the house might be a 'benitier', a decorative niche in a ground floor wall. Perhaps this was originally a piscina, filched from a church at the Reformation, or it may have been some form of domestic washing utensil. Normally ceilings were low, and from the kitchen's were hooks from which hung a wooden rack where salted bacon was kept. Nearby was the big open fireplace, originally housing a 'terpi', an iron tripod supporting the cooking pot, but later accommodating a Guernsey coal range. The bread oven would be in an adjacent wall in which apertures, or 'usettes', contained salt. There would be ample space for driftwood, 'kuapiaux' (dried cow dung pats), furze and vraic.

A characteristic piece of kitchen furniture was the green bed (la jonquière), a low, sturdy wooden structure on whose lathes were strewn bracken and, later, a mattress. This was a day-bed and the counterpart of a settee. The fine dresser contained much China, crockery and perhaps Guernsey christening cups of silver. Often the floor was earthen, with rushes or sand as a 'carpet'. The kitchen was far more used than the parlor, which was reserved for formal occasions, like weddings and funerals.

The farm outbuildings included stables, cowsheds, cartsheds, pigsties and barns, some of which had apertures in their gables for pigeons. A 'colombier' (dovecote) was the privilege of those seigneurs (lords of the manor) permitted to keep hundreds of birds in these structures. In the yard, or perhaps near an entrance, would be a stone mounting block. Sometimes these were built into the thickness of a wall.

Today, many Guernsey cattle roam the fields at will and often they have been de-horned. Formerly, animals were tethered (and many still are) so that the maximum of pasture was eaten before the beasts were staked elsewhere. Nowadays the tendency is to have a few large herds rather than several small ones. Hand-milking continues, often in the fields, although mechanical devices are common. Horses are no longer used for draught purposes, but many are employed for riding, particularly by children, so the sight of horses grazing is a common one, while that of the traditional Guernsey donkey has become a rarity.

A few sheep are still kept in Guernsey (there are more in Sark), but nothing like the numbers which grazed on L'Ancresse common until about 1920. Gates were set up here and there to prevent them from straying. A few goats are to be seen, notably those of the new Guernsey breed, and are often tethered on the island's cliffs and commons.

Circular and pointed ricks of harvested corn in sheaves awaiting threshing once stood on 'pilotins' (mushroom stones) in every stackyard. Hay ricks were also circular and small, but today they tend to be a mass of baled hay and, indeed, harvesting belongs to yesterday as far as pleasure is concerned. Likewise is the once familiar scene of a horse-drawn box-cart, laden with glistening vraic, being hauled up a stone slipway by a team of horses on the east or west coast. Today, it is rare for even a motor lorry to be so employed.

Windmills and watermills were once familiar objects in the Guernsey countryside. A few ruined towers survive, as well as some semi-derelict watermills, particularly in the King's Mills area. It was once a fine sight to see great horse-drawn loads of corn bound for the mills. Some of these were the property of the seigneurs. A watermill survives in Alderney and two windmill towers remain in Sark.

The Guernsey countryside is scarcely as it was a century ago. Then one beheld acres of crops under cultivation, as well as a multitude of green pastures, often shaded by belts of elm trees. Then farm workers wore smocks or guernseys, women wore 'scoop' bonnets, buildings were thatched and the horse prevailed, rather than today's tractor. A familiar sight was the forge, where horses were shod and implements repaired. The wheelwright plied his trade, like the coach-builder, and on every hand Guernsey-French was heard.

Today, while farms certainly exist, they are fewer and largely mechanised. Too many fields have become glasshouse sites and in our all-too-sparse countryside is an abundance of bungalows and other structures. Happily, a great many traditional buildings survive, all of which are modernised within, though their noble exteriors continue to grace their surroundings even if the chimneys are disfigured by television aerials! Thatch has gone, corrugated iron lingers, but often tiles make a welcome covering.

A host of mechanical vehicles have replaced the traditional wagons and the car has replaced the wagonette. Even so, what a welcome sight is often provided by the Guernsey Driving Club! One may still see a procession of horse-drawn conveyances on the roads of Guernsey (as one does in Sark) and, since riding has become such a popular pastime, the days of the horse are not yet over. The fine produce displayed in our markets and at agricultural shows proves that Guernsey's ancient industry is by no means dead.

59. (*above*) The coast at L'Erée, St. Peter-in-the-Wood, in about 1880. The nearest cottages have vanished, but those in the distance remain, together with the house which was the original L'Erée Hotel. The land on the sea side was used as a *sécage* for *vraic*. Dried seaweed was used extensively as fuel.

60. (*right*) Vraicing, or the gathering of seaweed, from the shore for use as fertilizer on the land. Large quantities of all types of drift weed, particularly the laminaries, were raked from the sea and carted to the land. Other weed was cut from the rocks with sickles. So great was the need for *vraic* for the economy of every farm that stringent laws were passed to ensure regular supplies.

61.   Cider making was carried on for centuries, and part of the process was the initial crushing of the apples in the circular stone trough, *le tour*, by means of a heavy stone wheel pulled around by an ox. Wooden wheels were more common and *le tour* was often inside a building and adjacent to the press, *l'emet*. The pole which extended from the central pivot to the animal served to guide it around the trough. The building in which the cider was made was *le prinseux*. About half a ton of apples would be crushed in a day, from which 100 gallons of cider would finally result.

62. Le Niaux mill, St. Andrew's, in about 1875, when the mill house was thatched and had a hipped gable. The mill race which fed water to the overshot wheel spanned a lane in a wooden aqueduct, supported on stone pillars.

63. The overshot water wheel at Le Niaux corn mill, St. Andrew's, frozen up during the great frost of 1895.

64 & 65. With the introduction of parsnips into island agriculture, deep ploughing was required. Thus *La Grande Charrue* or Big Plough came into use about the middle of the 18th century. It required at least eight animals to draw it and several farmers would co-operate. Each supplied one or more beasts as well as labourers. Oxen were once used by themselves, or with horses. Oxen had the greater pulling power at the end of the furrow, where it was always necessary to trench with a spade, *une bêque de Guernesi.* The collective effort also extended to breaks in the work for rest, food and drink for men and beasts brought to the field on horseback.

66. A horse and ox used together for the carting of hay in about 1900. The vehicle was a long cart.

67. Haymaking at Foulon Farm, St. Peter Port, in about 1890. The whole family, including grandma, is assembled with the farm workers.

68. Milking time at Duveaux Farm, St. Sampson's, in about 1900. Holding the cow is Mr. John Abraham Ogier. The milkmaid wearing a sun bonnet is Mrs. Le Tocq, who helped on the farm. Exports of Guernsey cattle to various parts of the world began in the 18th century. Americans were big customers, and of 1000 exported in 1914 some 800 went to the United States.

69. (*right*) Butter making at Duveaux Farm, St. Sampson's, in about 1900. Fresh milk was poured into earthenware crocks and curdled milk added. When coagulated, it was poured into the churn, in this case a standing barrel type. Warm water was added while churning and later the lumps of butter were rinsed with cold water, salted and worked to give a fine texture. After weighing into pats the butter was placed on the farm's own wooden stamp, which gave it a label, fluted by hand and gently rested on a cabbage leaf.

70. An ox-drawn box-cart at St. Peter-in-the-Wood in about 1908. It was a little shorter than the long cart. Minus shafts and fitted with rubber tyres, it is still used on farms. The cart, built with heavier wood, was used extensively in island quarries.

71. Sheep once grazed on L'Ancresse common and at the beginning of the 20th century (and even later) this was a familiar sight. Until well into the century gates barred the approaches to the Common to prevent animals from straying. Until 1806 this part of Guernsey—still known as Le Clos du Valle—was separated from its parent by a sea channel, Le Braye du Valle, which was reclaimed, mainly in the interests of the island's defence.

VI

ST. PETER PORT

Viewed from the sea, Guernsey's capital makes an engaging picture. There is Castle Cornet, with the green heights of Fort George beyond it. Rising in tiers from the spacious harbour, the old town presents a scene which, superficially at all events, is not very dissimilar from that of a century ago. Houses clothe the hillside and, as a backcloth, the towers of St. Peter Port seem to mount guard on the skyline.

Their silhouettes comprise the former church of St. Barnabas, St. Joseph's steeple, the pinnacles of Elizabeth College, St. James's church and Victoria Tower. Their finials complete a scene of character and comeliness which, in its way, has no peer in the Channel Islands; yet all these buildings are 19th century creations. Of the same era is Castle Carey, embowered in trees and flanked by the verdant estate of Les Côtils.

The stranger arriving by sailing packet very early in the last century would have beheld a skyline dominated only by L'Hyvreuse windmill (now supplanted by Victoria Tower) with the houses of New Town on the left, and the buildings overlooking the New Ground (later renamed Cambridge Park, after the visit of the Duke of Cambridge in 1862) on the right. The trees of Les Côtils would have terminated the prospect northwards, as they still do.

If we take the dawn of photography in the island as being about 1850, the picture of the town as observed from the sea would have largely resembled today's, save that St. Joseph's spire was not finished until 1885 and St. Barnabas' church dates from 1874, so that these would have been absent. Otherwise, most of today's quayside and hillside buildings were standing in the middle of the last century.

The port, however, looked very different then. It originally comprised what used to be styled the Old Harbour (now the Victoria yacht marina) and it was not until the 1850s that the New Harbour was built. Castle Cornet was on an isolated rock until it was joined to the 'mainland' at that period, while the North and South Esplanades also date from the middle of the 19th century.

It is fortunate that photography had reached Guernsey by the time of the harbour's enlargement, since several valuable pictures were taken of this major undertaking. Unhappily, photographers paid less attention to the development of St. Sampson's harbour at about the same period. Probably the metamorphosis of the greater haven overshadowed that of the lesser.

In an old town, as in any ancient setting, the presence of antique forms of transport adds to the scene's appeal. Thus to see horse-drawn vehicles lumbering over the stone setts of St. Peter Port was more harmonious than the sight of motor transport in its narrow streets. Certainly modern conveyances are inevitable, but from the eye of the artist they are still incongruous under these conditions (unless deliberate contrast is sought).

While much of the town's architecture is of the 19th century and the bulk of it survives, at the same time certain areas have been subjected to drastic change, and this especially applies to the surroundings of the Town Church. Several old buildings have been demolished to give it greater dignity and more light, and this demolition included the inns on its eastern side in 1914.

Cornet Street is another place where much-needed alterations were carried out, and to compare its appearance in 1900 with that of 1977 is to appreciate what changes have been wrought in the interests of safety and hygiene. It has lost much of its former quaint appearance and, happily, all of its evil atmosphere. Le Bordage, likewise, has been widened and several of its old buildings demolished in the process. Photographs of these recall the Victorian scene.

Usually, old illustrations of town and harbour are now esteemed more than those of the cliffs which, in the main, have changed but little. Close scrutiny, though, will reveal that today these heights are more densely vegetated than hitherto; obviously some buildings have gone and others have periodically replaced them.

Views of the outskirts of St. Peter Port as they used to be are of value, since no commercial photographer troubles about them today. One thinks of cards showing Les Banques, the Bouet, the Ivy Gates, the environs of Fort George and some of the town's lanes and flights of steps. The appearance of trams, buses and other conveyances also enhances their worth.

A colourful aspect of island life was the presence of the military in and around St. Peter Port. Troops were stationed at Castle Cornet and Fort George, the Militia was often seen and periodically there were changes of garrison. All these movements were captured by the lens and particularly the great review at Fort George on the Sovereign's birthday. Likewise, the visits of royalty and other notables were so recorded.

Cavalcades, civic occasions, funerals of the exalted, sports meetings, fetes and outings all came under the eye of the photographer. New ships at St. Peter Port, regattas, stately yachts, prosaic merchantmen and fishing craft were not overlooked; and today, in private and public collections, these souvenirs of yesterday are rightly cherished.

In the section of 'Ships and Harbours' this aspect of island photography has been dealt with more particularly, but in any survey of Guernsey's capital its port and vessels are bound to be mentioned. Its importance is not confined to this facet, though, for St. Peter Port is the seat of local government and the dispensation of justice, as well as being the major shopping centre. The photographer of the past did not cast a blind eye on the salient factors of the town and parish and, thanks to him, we are able to appreciate what has happened over the past century—which the best of artists could scarcely have equalled.

However pleasing a town, harbour or group of buildings may be, they are, after all, but settings for the people using them. In the 19th and early part of the 20th century the people were colourful not so much in their attire as in their pursuits and foibles. One recalls Jack Trump, who must have been one of the best-known island figures of his time. A knife-grinder by trade (who operated a foot-propelled contrivance), he was also the unofficial town crier. It is said he was illiterate, since he often 'read' his script upside down, but he claimed to be an artist, even though his paintings were as peculiar as the rest of him.

There were the lamplighters who, at dusk, were to be seen about the streets with long poles, with which the gas lights were turned on. Their meeting-place was under the arch in High Street. French onion-sellers were familiar sights and so were roadsweepers. Elderly islanders may remember the German band which played in St. Peter Port before the First World War. At Christmas, carol singers were numerous.

There was more music from the blind organ-grinder who, on Saturdays, played at the top of the Market steps. At other times he was heard elsewhere. Occasionally, military bands were seen and heard as they played on the march. Such sounds, together with the beat of horses' hooves, were more pleasing to the ear than today's din from traffic and aircraft.

Often milk was delivered by donkey cart and served direct from churn to jug. The sight of coalmen in their horse-drawn carts was a common one, like that of men pushing hand trucks, and errand boys, with their big baskets, whistling the latest 'hits' and not above joining in street games with their younger brethren. And it was always interesting to wander in the vicinity of Trinity Square and watch blacksmiths at work or to peer into the bus stables.

Less agreeable was the presence of ragged children and to see poor folk gathering coal on the Quay. Too often one observed drunken men in the hands of the police and sometimes drivers were brutal to their horses. There were marked differences between rich and poor: how extreme was the contrast between the homes of the wealthy in the Grange and Queen's Road, and the wretched poverty of the houses in Pedvin Street and Rosemary Lane!

A handful of police maintained order in St. Peter Port and they were maintained by the parish. A few States police patrolled the rest of the island, together with the parochial constables. The fire engine was a noble, horse-drawn equipage, complete with clanging bell and brass-helmeted firemen clinging on like grim death! In very hot weather water carts operated in the dusty streets, and sometimes straw was laid in the road outside the home of a sick person, to deaden the sounds of traffic.

On every hand the sound of 'Guernsey-English' was to be heard, and this peculiar dialect (often a literal translation from the French), with its inimitable intonation, has become almost obsolete. Radio and television have helped to kill it (as they have slain the patois) and their aerials mar so many buildings in town and countryside today.

72. St. Peter Port under construction in about 1857. The tall chimney on the right of the Town Church is the contractors' mortar mill. Other buildings connected with the harbour works are standing on what is now the omnibus terminus.

73. St. Peter Port as it appeared in 1885. Guernsey fishing boats lie at anchor and on the left the steamer *Serk* is berthed at the Albert Pier. Sailing ships are in the Old Harbour. Today this area is devoted to yacht marinas.

74. Vauvert, St. Peter Port, as it looked 80 years ago. Many of the buildings remain, but horse-drawn traffic has gone, like the hand trucks and wheelbarrows drawn by errand boys.

75. This ancient group of houses, making the corner of Fountain Street in Church Square and west of the Town Church, was pulled down in 1874 to make way for the Lower Vegetable Market, completed in 1879. The corner house bordering Fountain Street and Church Square formerly belonged to the Carey family, having been bought by Perrin Careye in 1429. The central building is that of N. L. Lihou's tea and coffee house.

76. A section of the North Beach, now part of the North Esplanade, in about 1856. Marshall's Royal Yacht Hotel is where Sir Isaac Brock, 'The Saviour of Canada', lived. This is now Boots' premises. Renier's Hotel is now the Crown Hotel, and among other old buildings on the right is J. & T. Snow, sailmakers, and James Jeune, cabinet-maker. In the foreground is the Victoria Pier.

77. Gardner's Royal Hotel as it appeared in about 1900. Its annexe, seen on the right, was later rebuilt and incorporated in the main building. On the left, Bohn's establishment was acquired and formed a wing of the 'Royal'. The original building was once Le Grand Bosq, the town residence of the Le Marchant family, whose country seat was at Les Grandes Maisons, St. Sampson's.

78. St. James's Street as it appeared in about 1850. The buildings include the former police station, dated 1888, which was demolished in 1955. The Greffe Office, built in about 1846, is not in the picture. Today the site is occupied by the offices of the Crown officers and police headquarters.

79. Bordage Street photographed in about 1880. None of the stores and shops on the left now exist. Note the curiosity of the bystanders and the absence of traffic.

80. Fountain Street after the completion of the Fish Market in 1877. The street was still cobbled and the upper part had not yet been widened. Up the street on the left was Noel and de la Rue's household ironmongery business, where Guernsey milk cans were also manufactured.

81. Le Grand Carrefour, High Street, St. Peter Port, in about 1875. A lamp over the arch leading to the Constables' Office bears the inscription: 'Soldiers' Institute' and a notice on the right declares: 'J. W. Jones, Engraver. Entrance round the corner'. The paving remains, but not the attractive design in the foreground, unfortunately.

82. This area of Le Bordage, St. Peter Port, was known as 'Cheapside' in the last century. The firm of J. Le Page, clock makers, was founded in 1780. Next door was J. S. Head's bakery, where bread was baked in hot air ovens, 'the most up to date that science has produced', it was claimed.

83. William H. De La Mare's haberdashery at Le Petit Carrefour, Bordage, in about 1905.

84. Le Petit Carrefour, or 'Top of the Market', before the double-fronted shop premises were demolished. Nicolle's shop and tearoom remained until after 1945, when it too was rebuilt. Nicolle's Guernsey sweets were famous.

85. (below) A busy scene in Market Square in about 1910. On the left, an organ-grinder stands beside a horse, wrapped in a blanket to keep out the cold. Other animals and their vehicles fill the square, while Edwardian shoppers go about their business sedately.

The Market Square, Guernsey.

86.   St. Julian's Hall was built in
1876 at a cost of £2,000 as an Odd
Fellows' Hall. In 1885 it was enlarged
at a cost of £1,800 and in 1914 it became St. Julian's Theatre. Seats for
the 'Two Grand Concerts', being bill-
ed when the photograph was taken,
cost five francs and three francs. The
building is now the Gaumont Cinema.

87.   (below) On 12 October 1911,
the first annual outing of the manager,
staff and friends of St. Julian's Theatre
took place. The group is posed outside
the building.

88. The top of Grange Road, St. Peter Port, at 12.45 p.m. on 16 July 1913. At the corner of Brock Road is a bus horse with a boy rider up. The animal was used as a leader on the Victoria Road hill by the buses running from the Market Place to Cobo. Varna House, behind the horse, was purchased by the States and demolished in August 1915. Today, the midday scene there is very different!

89. The Maritime Inn and People's Café on the east side of the Town Church were demolished in 1914. There was no traffic to disturb the photographer, whose wife provided the human interest!

90. (*above*) Cornet Street from Church Square in February 1914, shortly before the bottom of the street was altered and steps provided. Bucktrout & Company occupied the building on the east side of the street and it was there they had their tobacco factory. The former States Office stood on the western corner.

91. (*left*) Figuring prominently in this picture is the saddlery and shoeing forge of James Saunders, in Trinity Square, St. Peter Port. The photograph was taken in about 1880.

92. Until 1920 the Constables and Douzaine of St. Peter Port were responsible for ensuring that police duties were carried out in the Town parish. In 1853 the parish had four paid policemen; later they were increased to twelve. This photograph was taken in about 1908 and shows the two Constables, Messrs. O. Priaulx and W. de P. Crousaz, seated in the centre. The policemen are, left to right, George Boucher, Cliff Tardif, Jim Marley, Frank Pulsford, Lance Corporal Fred Roberts, Jim Ley, Frank Adams, Sergeant George Burley, Sam Gallienne, Fred Le Poidevin, Sam Lanford and Frank Delsey.

VII

SOCIAL AND COMMUNAL LIFE

It is sometimes wondered what Victorians did with their leisure: the answer is that not many had very much to enjoy. The well-to-do were not usually idle, for their tastes were for the arts and the sciences; even on holiday they normally set out to improve their minds, as guide-book writers of the era remembered. The working class, to use the contemporary term, laboured for so long and for so little that the small amount of time they had for themselves was often either spent in resting or perhaps gardening.

Yet life was not all work and no play and in the country, especially, it was often arranged that labour and leisure were combined. Passing reference has been made to 'La Grande Querue', the big plough used for the cultivation of parsnips. A feast followed its employment, since the farmer concerned was expected to feed his helpers, who worked without fee. Victuals were not confined to the day's end, for there were pauses for rest and refreshment at 10 a.m. lunch (bread and butter, cheese, dried cod and strong tea), dinner (cabbage soup, ham and pork), tea (with gâche) and finally supper, with more beef, ham, plum pudding and unlimited cider. For good measure there was singing, dancing, story-telling and games, to which the relatives of the ploughmen were invited.

When Guernsey folk went sand-eeling it was accompanied by a degree of enjoyment, apart from the pleasure of the expedition itself. After the fish had been disturbed they were caught as they leaped to the surface of the sand in such bays as Vazon, Grandes Rocques, L'Ancresse and Petit Port. Sand-eels are still enjoyed as food as well as being used as bait.

Vraic-gathering provided pleasure also, as well as labour. Young people adorned their hats with flowers, nosegays ornamented the horses' heads, and there was competition as everyone, young and old, tried to gather as much cut weed as possible while the tide permitted. Some took advantage of conditions to go ormering, using 'hooks' to prise these delicious univalves from rocks far below ordinary tide level. Crabbing was also indulged in. At last all the shore-gatherers assembled on the dunes to enjoy a picnic, before the vraic was carted off to farmyards or spread on drying grounds near the beach. Sometimes their day was rounded off by dancing.

More sedate was the custom of 'La Môme': a girl was chosen by residents of a district on Midsummer Day, who sat on the 'lit de fouaille' or 'la jonquière' (a green bed or rustic divan in the kitchen), which was richly decorated with flowers, arranged as garlands. Fern was strewn over the floor and, while the guests did homage, the girl sat silent and in state. This was a curious custom.

In the last century the countryman went to town on at least two occasions: on Christmas Eve and on the Queen's birthday. The last was compulsory for all male islanders, since they were members of the Royal Guernsey Militia which, on the royal birthday, paraded with the garrison at Belvedere Field, Fort George, for the grand review by the Lieutenant-Governor. It was a most colourful spectacle and the day itself was a public holiday.

So was New Year's Day (it remains so, happily), when official receptions were held by His Excellency and by the Bailiff, among other notabilities. In Alderney, to this day, the Fire Brigade has a practice drill in Marais Square on 1 January, and it is the custom for the watching crowd to 'dare' the firemen to spray them with their hoses, which they do with gusto. Another special Alderney custom is known as 'Milk-a-punch Sunday', held in May, when the pubs offer a punch made of rum and milk to all callers for nothing. One glass per caller is, however, the rule.

A Sark custom of unknown age is still kept in Sark on Good Friday. It is the sailing of model boats on Beauregard Pond. A charming Sark observance follows a wedding, when the bride and groom drive round the island distributing wine and cake to those unable to attend the ceremony. On Midsummer Day in Sark it was usual to decorate horses and carriages and drive about in festive mood.

The burning of Guy Fawkes' effigy on 5 November has long been a custom in the Guernsey Bailiwick. The guy is known as a 'budloe', because, once upon a time, it was usual to burn the remains of the Yule log on New Year's Eve, the log being called 'le bout de l'an' (the end of the year). The expression was transferred to the guy, and it is still a term of disrespect when someone is likened to a 'budloe'. It was formerly the habit of the people of St. Martin's to arrange a grand procession on 5 November, with several 'budloes' riding in carriages, the cavalcade being headed by a band. It marched (if that is the word) to town and back again and the guys were then committed to the flames.

Sport in Guernsey was enjoyed in the last century, particularly shooting. This was especially useful to the Militiamen who, as well as carrying out manoeuvres on L'Ancresse common, used it for musketry. Remains of the butts are still visible. Others were at Vazon and Grandes Rocques. The Militiamen had more sport when they were in camp at Les Beaucamps, and the Militia band was often heard on the march.

Golf has been popular on L'Ancresse common since the links were made there in the last century. In its early days, especially, cycling was greatly enjoyed, and the football pitch known as 'The Track' was originally made for bicycle racing. Walking races, rambles (and particularly cliff walks) were other forms of recreation enjoyed in Guernsey, as well as the conventional football and cricket.

For the music-lover, there were the excellent concerts given by the Guille-Alles choral and orchestral society and the performances at Candie Gardens by the bands of the garrison and Militia in Summer. There, too, concert parties provided entertainment on fine evenings. In bad weather performances were held at St. George's Hall, a big place originally built for roller-skating. Exhibitions were also held there.

Theatrical shows were to be attended at St. Julian's Hall, below which was the Pillar Hall, used for dancing. Early cinema performances were held at St. Julian's, Rectory House and the Lyric Hall, while variety shows were available at 'Billy Bartlett's', otherwise 'The Palace of Varieties'. All over the island, fetes, bazaars and similar functions were as general a century ago as they still are. There were lectures, too, as well as excursions by the Guernsey Society of Natural Science and Local Research (now La Société Guernesiaise), while photographic clubs, sketching parties and organised walks were popular.

Tourists drove about the island in 'four-in-hands', high vehicles drawn by four horses, and islanders often made summer excursions in jubilee cars, brakes, wagonettes and similar horse-drawn conveyances. The more daring went by cycle. By modern standards, much of this entertainment would be deemed childish and unsophisticated, but to the Victorian and Edwardian islander it was fun and a welcome break from the many hours of sheer hard work and a low wage which, today, would be regarded with equal distaste.

93. A west coast scene in the 1870s. Poor, barefooted children such as these would run from their cottages, demanding 'des doubles, des doubles' — money from visitors conveyed around the island in open horse-drawn excursion cars.

94. The kitchen of a Guernsey cottage in about 1906. Above the fireplace is the bacon rack, and beside it is the dresser. Fuel is on the left and the kitchen table is by the window. The woman is wearing a 'scoop' bonnet.

95. Cobo Hotel, Castel, a favourite west coast halt for wagonette parties in the 1880s. It stood below Le Guet.

96. St. Saviour's cavalcade, showing the participants assembling at Les Caches. The year was 1898, when penny postage was introduced.

97. L'Ancresse common in 1873. Here the Guernsey Rifle Association met for their annual competitions. The event was also an excuse for family outings.

98. Guernsey winners of the Kolapore Cup at Bisley in 1890. Standing: Lt. Col. J. Leale and Miss W. L. Leale. Seated, centre: Sgt. T. Albigès, Pte. D. Le Poidevin, Pte. E. Despointes, Cpl. M. King, Sgt. J. Smith, Sgt. T. Aldridge. Front: Cpl. A. Jory and Cpl. J. Falla.

99. Members of the Reliance Air Rifle Shooting Club team, winners of the shield in about 1912. They had a range at Le Pontac, Vazon.

100. The Guernsey Archery Club, c.1880. Presumably the ladies' elegant attire did not interfere with their prowess with the bow.

101.   These people had cycled about seven miles from St. Peter Port to Rocquaine for an outing on the west coast. Behind is a horse-drawn wagonette with another party aboard.

102.   Cycling, towards the end of the last century, was a very popular sport in Guernsey. Some of these riders have 'penny farthing' machines. They are standing below Victoria Tower, and in the background is the Town Arsenal.

103. St. Saviour's Coronation Fête, 1911. King Edward VII died in 1910 and was succeeded by George V, whose coronation was celebrated in the following year. Three types of bicycle appear in the picture.

104. Guy Fawkes celebrations in about 1900. For many years the St. Martinais organised a march around the parish on 5 November. This procession assembled at the Duke of York Hotel, later Le Dain's bakery, then the Hotel Beaulieu and now the Carlton Hotel. The procession was headed by a volunteer fife and drum band, and hundreds of people followed it to its final destination, where Guy Fawkes was hanged on a gibbet.

105. Participants in St. Martin's 'Old Guernsey Bazaar', which took place at Easter 1907. Men dressed in former Militia uniform are seen with the clergy. The fete was a most ambitious affair.

106. In about 1910 roller-skating was all the rage in Guernsey. Some of those gathered at St. George's Hall have hockey sticks. The building was also used for exhibitions, dancing and concerts.

107. The Gaieties at Candie Gardens, 1906. Formerly concert parties were summer attractions in Guernsey and were performed on the bandstand in fine weather, and when the elements were unkind, at St. George's Hall. The 'troupes', as they were called, usually stayed for a week, when they were replaced by others.

108. St. Julian's Theatre, St. Peter Port, with members of the Guille-Alles Choral and Orchestral Association. Photographed in 1909, it shows S. Coleridge-Taylor sitting in the front, third from right. He conducted his composition, 'Hiawatha', before a packed audience.

109. The French poet and novelist, Victor Hugo, who spent over 14 years in exile in Guernsey between 1856 and 1870 at his home, Hauteville House, St. Peter Port. The photograph is by Garnier Arsène, who lived in St. James's Street.

110. (*above*) John Oxenham, the novelist, resided in Sark in the early years of the present century, and here some of his delightful island stories were written. They were 'Carette of Sark', 'Pearl of Pearl Island', 'A Maid of the Silver Sea' and 'The Perilous Lovers'. He also collaborated with the artist, William Toplis, in bringing out 'The Book of Sark', limited to 500 copies.

THE TOWN CRIER, GUERNSEY. F. W. Guerin. Photo.

111. (*right*) Jack Trump, Guernsey's town crier, in about 1907. He was a familiar figure in the streets of St. Peter Port, where he also operated a knife-grinding machine.

GUERNSEY. — Saint Peter Port - The White Rock. — II
for the Mail Boat. — Saint Pierre Port. - Sur la Jetée. —

112. For those with leisure, 'going down to the boat' was a favourite pastime about 70 years ago. In those days, spectators visiting the White Rock could climb onto an elevated platform, known by some as 'the bandstand', beside the Spur lighthouse. It was demolished during the German Occupation.

113. The beach at Rocquaine around the year 1902, showing Fort Grey in the background. Juvenile sports are in progress.

114.   The staff of La Haye du Puits, Castel, in about 1900. The house is one of the finest in Guernsey.

115.   Taken on a beach near le Chouet, Vale, this picture shows the staff of the Guernsey Electric Light & Power Company Limited enjoying their annual outing in about 1910. Ten years earlier electricity was first used in Guernsey by Mr. A. P. Roger in his Commercial Arcade premises. The first electricity station was at Les Amballes, and in 1904 the generating station at North Side, Vale, was opened to provide power for the stone works nearby. In 1932 the firm was taken over by the States of Guernsey.

116.   The Forest School 'Mixed' Group Three, taken in 1905.

117. Swimming sports at Petit Bôt in 1911. A wooden diving platform was bolted to the rocks for the occasion and the officials were ferried to the rocks by boat. Lounge suits and 'boaters' were popular in those days.

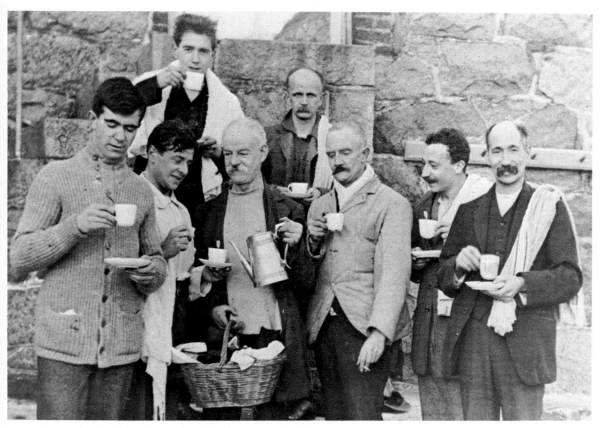

118. After the swim the coffee. Christmas Day 1913, at the Gentlemen's Pool, La Vallette. Front: G. Cleversley, E. Luff, — King, Major Myles, C. Toms, P. Etor. Back: S. Green, — Clarke.

With Best Wishes

119.   The Guernsey States telephone exchange first opened for traffic on 28 July 1898 in the former Clifton chapel, Clifton, St. Peter Port, where this photograph of the 'Hello Girls' was taken in 1914.

120.   A 1913 tricar, built by Mr. William Green, a cycle dealer of Smith Street, St. Peter Port. Seated at the wheel is Miss Daisy Green, with her mother, Mrs. Emma Green, and young Bill (now Deputy W. Green) seated on her lap.

121. This archway, at the foot of Victoria Road, was set up on 10 March 1888. 'God save Albert and Alexandra' referred to the Prince of Wales and his Princess. Today this scene has changed completely.

122. Mrs. Margaret Anne Neve, born in 1792, photographed in her 109th year. She enjoyed the unique experience of living in three centuries: the 18th, 19th and 20th. Mrs. Neve married on 18 January 1823 and she and her husband spent their honeymoon visiting (among other places) Waterloo eight years after the battle. She resided at Rouge Huis, St. Peter Port, and died on 4 April 1903, six weeks before her 111th birthday. Her grave is in Le Cimetière des Frères, St. Peter Port.

m a neve 1792 1901

(Written by Mrs Neve May 26ᵗʰ 1901. a week after her 109ᵗʰ birthday. E.T.C.)

123. On 22 July 1899, Private William A. Priaulx, of the 1st Royal Guernsey Light Infantry, won the Queen's Prize at Bisley, after one of the closest and most exciting contests on record. He had always been a good shot. At the Guernsey Rifle Association meeting in 1891 he was the winner of the Lieutenant Governor's Prize, and for many years he was the best shot of the regiment. In accordance with established custom, he was 'chaired' and carried around the camp, followed by an enthusiastic crowd.

124. A meeting of the court of the Fief d'Anneville in the porch of Anneville House, near Le Camp du Roi, early in the present century. The Fiefs des Anneville et de Fauville were acquired by Henry III in 1248. They were purchased by Professor C. Northcote Parkinson in 1964, and this was the first time they had changed hands since 1509. Because of the ruinous condition of the manor house the court met in its porch until 1977, when the present Seigneur completed its restoration and the court met inside the building.

125. A meeting of La Cour du Fief Beuval at Les Sages, St. Pierre du Bois, in about 1900. Officials are seated on a stone bench in the garden of the house, while the tenants are standing nearby. One of the court officers is taking an oath, administered by the Seneschal.

126.   Rain, apparently, did not stop the ceremony of inaugurating the statue of Prince Albert on 8 October 1863, although the sea of umbrellas prevented the photographer from seeing much of what was happening.

127.   On the death of Queen Victoria in 1901, her Diamond Jubilee statue in Candie Grounds was dressed in mourning and its base was covered with wreaths. The statue, unveiled in 1900, was by C. B. Birch and is a replica of the original at Bombay.

128.   A royal occasion in 1905, when the Duke of Connaught visited Guernsey and unveiled the South African War Memorial in St. Julian's Avenue. He is seen here in a motor car, driving up Grange Road in company with the Lieutenant-Governor.

129.   In 1905 the Duke of Connaught (centre) visited Guernsey, primarily to unveil the South African War Memorial in St. Julian's Avenue. On his right is the Lieutenant-Governor, Major-General B. B. D. Campbell. The photograph was taken at His Excellency's residence, Saumarez Park.

130.   The swearing-in of Major-General R. Auld as Lieutenant-Governor of Guernsey in the Royal Court in April 1908. The Bailiff was Sir Henry Giffard K. C.

131.   The impressive military funeral of the Lieutenant-Governor, Major-General R. Auld, in February 1911. The service was held at St. Joseph's Church and the cortège is seen entering Queen's Road, on its way to the military cemetery at Fort George, where he was buried. It is rare for a Lieutenant-Governor to die in office in Guernsey.

132. (*right*) Between 1808 and 1813, when England and Sweden were about the only countries which had not been conquered by Napoleon, Admiral Sir James Saumarez' fleet blockaded Copenhagen and soon had complete control of the Danish warships. Saumarez' task was to defend Sweden while blockading the hostile coast of Denmark, Prussia and Russia, and at the same time protecting the English and Swedish merchantmen. After Saumarez' death it was decided to honour his memory by erecting a monument on the heights of Delancey, St. Sampson's. The foundation stone was laid on 1 August 1876. This picture was taken in 1877.

133. (*below*) On 22 May 1910, the Swedish Government sent two warships to Guernsey, under Count G. A. Wachmeister, commanding officer of the cruiser *Fylgia*, who placed a wreath at the memorial. Attached to the base of the obelisk were four bronze plaques, one of which bore the effigy of Lord de Saumarez. The monument was destroyed by the German occupying forces on 7 December 1943.

134. (*above*) The proclamation of King
George V on the Royal Court terrace in
May 1910. The Lieutenant-Governor is
leading the cheers for His Majesty, after
the proclamation has been read by H. M.
Sheriff, standing at the flag-draped rostrum.
Members of the Royal Court and States
throng the terrace, below which is the
guard of honour.

135. (*right*) High Street, St. Peter Port,
en fête. The decorations are probably for
the coronation of Edward VII and consist
mainly of Chinese lanterns.

136. Guernsey were the 1907 winners of the Muratti Cup against Jersey, 3 — 2 after extra time. This inter-insular event has been played — except for war-time interruptions — since 1905. The team: Aubert, Waterman, Parry (capt.), Cooper, F. Stranger, Mahy, Yates, Stocker, T. Leadbeater, Holland, Thorne.

137. On 2 July 1905, Martello tower No. 1 was blown up at Hougue à la Perre when the hillock was levelled. This assisted tram cars on their journey between Town and St. Sampson's. The coast road then passed between the battery and the tram sheds. Close by, First Tower Lane still serves as a reminder of the first of such towers to be built in Guernsey about two hundred years ago.

138. The seaward side of Braye Street, Alderney, as it appeared in about 1890. The houses' basements adjoin a quay, now completely covered by sand. A pilot boat is at Douglas Quay and in the roadstead is H.M. gunboat *Raven.*

139. Torpedo boats and other warships anchored in the Alderney roadstead during the naval manoeuvres of 1901. The destroyer *Viper* struck rocks off Burhou in dense fog and became a total loss, though all aboard were saved.

140.   The *Courier* approaching the landing stage at Braye harbour, Alderney, in 1905. She was built in 1883 for the Alderney Steam Packet Company for the mail service between Guernsey and Alderney. She also plied to Sark. A splendid little vessel, she served the islands until 1940, when she was engaged on war service. The ship made a welcome return for a further period in 1945. In April 1906, while returning from Sark to St. Peter Port, she foundered off Les Anons, south of Jethou, with the loss of 10 lives. At a court of enquiry her master, Captain N. Whales, was found guilty of negligence. The picture shows her going astern into her berth.

141.   The *Courier* at the breakwater slipway in 1890. She berthed there in the days before the jetty was built. In the background is Fort Albert. Troops of the garrison are in the foreground.

142. Platte Saline, Alderney, in about 1900. The building in the foreground is Picaterre Brewery. Beyond it is Fort Platte Saline and steaming up the Swinge, with steadying sails hoisted, is the *Courier*. Burhou lies in the background.

143. When John Wesley visited Alderney in 1787 he stayed at what is now the Diver's Inn, where the 'X' above the sign marks his bedroom. The person behind the cart is Bob Allen, the harbourmaster.

144. (*right*) The top of Victoria Street,
Alderney, in 1900. The fashions have changed,
but on the whole this important road is much as
it was, in terms of architecture. The stone setts
remain, as well as the Victorian shopfronts and
trees.

145. (*below*) Victoria Street, Alderney, was
gaily beflagged in 1905, when the Duke of
Connaught visited the island. In his honour
St. Anne's Square was renamed Royal
Connaught Square. Victoria Street still looks
much the same as it did when the Duke was
there.

146. Victoria Street, Alderney, had a rather more peaceful appearance in 1912 than it has today, when it is partly a one-way thoroughfare. On the left is the site of the Albert Inn; opposite, the Chez André Hotel replaces the former Andover House and the Post Office beside it.

147. Le Huret, Alderney, in about 1906. As usual at that period, the presence of a photographer attracted great attention and people made a point of being in the picture.

148.   Clonque Cottage, Alderney, in 1906. This charming building, now modernised but still unspoilt, stands beside the coast road running past Fort Tourgis to Fort Clonque, on the north-west coast of the island. Behind the building the land rises to the Little Blaye. These were former pastures which have now been considerably built upon.

149.   The Valley, Alderney, photographed in 1910. By the pump is a box-cart; the horse may have drunk at the trough nearby. Beside it is the gateway of the Terrace, as wooded as this road leading down to Crabby.

150.   In the days before the First World War, Alderney cattle were in considerable demand overseas, and this photograph shows animals in Marais Square awaiting shipment in a small vessel before being transferred to a bigger one. The cattle were assembled in the square and then led down to the harbour. The existence of a distinct breed of Alderney cattle is disbelieved by some authorities, who declare that the Alderney and Guernsey cow are one and the same. This photograph was taken in 1912.

151.   The wrecked full-rigged ship *Liverpool* off the eastern tip of Alderney in 1902. The largest sailing vessel in the world at the time, she struck the rocks in dense fog because her master thought she was off Les Casquets instead of nine miles further east. Happily, no lives were lost, but efforts to refloat the ship proved fruitless; after a few days she foundered, but not before much of her valuable cargo had been removed. The photograph, taken by Thomas Westness, shows the ship off Fort Hommeaux Florains, still with all sails set.

152.   Mannez lighthouse, Alderney, under construction in 1912. Beyond is Fort Les Hommeaux Florains, near which the full-rigger *Liverpool* was lost in 1902. Because of the number of wrecks off this part of the coast the lighthouse was built.

153. A steamer loading stone at Cachalière pier, Alderney, in about 1910. It was quarried and crushed nearby, at the foot of high cliffs, and the stone was transported to the pierhead for shipment. Today the pier and adjacent buildings are derelict.

Wreck off Alderney—"Petite Raymond," 1906.
Copyright.

154. The wreck of the French schooner *Petit Raymond* in 1906. She went aground near the site of the Alderney lighthouse; beyond her is the grave of the *Liverpool*.

155. Creux Harbour in about 1880. Several early attempts at building a breakwater to enclose La Motte Bay failed, and it was not until 1822 that they finally succeeded. But the wall was breached in 1866 and had to be rebuilt, this time wider and stronger. The break in the wall, over which a bridge was constructed, was to allow for the surge of water, but this gap was later filled in.

156. The paddle steamer *Rescue II* moored at Les Laches, off Creux Harbour. In 1878 this new steam tug arrived in Guernsey to replace the former tug of that name. Both were used on excursions to Sark, as well as for towing.

157. In 1906 Harry Turner resolved to post himself from Guernsey to Sark, to which the GPO agreed at that time. With its permission therefore, a person might be delivered to a destination by Royal Mail, accompanied by a Post Office telegraph messenger. Both are seen aboard the Sark boat; on arrival Mr. Turner and his escort went for a drive, lunched at Dixcart Hotel and later returned to Guernsey, having made island history.

158. A Sark family outside their thatched cottage. This 19th century photograph shows the fashions of the period and the rather primitive appearance of the island's dwellings. Thatched buildings no longer grace the scene, unhappily.

159.   The road up from Creux harbour, Sark. The scene is much as it was when it was photographed in about 1900, although box-carts have given way to tractors. The trees remain, and carriages still use this charming gateway to the island.

160.   Avenue House, Sark, still stands at La Collinette, though the space between it and the wall is now a tearoom. The Avenue gate has gone, like most of the trees, and today there are shops and much traffic along this hitherto quiet road.

161.   La Friponnerie, Sark, now the site of the Bel Air bar and restaurant. The cottages were thatched at the turn of the century. The thatch has disappeared and cows are no longer milked in the forecourt.

162.   The Bel Air Hotel, Sark, which the Germans destroyed during the Occupation. It stood at La Collinette, at the top of the harbour hill, and comprised an old thatched building and a more modern wing, seen on the right. This photograph dates from about 1910.

163. L'Ecluse, Sark, with James Hamon, the miller, at the door. This charming thatched cottage, now a hotel, stands in a wooded valley near La Seigneurie. The mill, not far off, is disused and less attractive than it was in its heyday. This picture must be nearly a century old.

164. Cottages at La Fregondeé, on Sark's west coast. The buildings remain and are still charming, even though they lack the thatch and rustic appearance they enjoyed in 1905, when this picture was taken.

165. La Seigneurie grounds early in the present century. Known as the Battery, this enclosure has several old cannon, the best of which is the Elizabethan saker on the right. It was presented by Elizabeth I to the first Seigneur of Sark, Helier de Carteret, and the inscription on its bronze surface is still to be discerned. The other guns in the picture are of the 18th century.

166. Sark's present Seigneurie was originally built in 1565 and was then known as La Perronerie. It was rebuilt in 1675 and in 1854 a new wing was added, as well as the tower, seen here under construction.

167. La Coupée, Sark, is about two hundred yards long, narrow and at one time a dangerous isthmus, joining Big Sark with Little Sark. It is 260 feet above sea level and before protective railings were erected in 1900 it was often a hazardous crossing in bad weather. In 1731 a man was blown off the road to his death and, much later, children are said to have had to crawl across to reach the school in Big Sark when a gale was blowing. Several landslides have occured, which reduced its width in 1811 and 1862. Its savage grandeur is captured in this picture, taken in about 1900.

168. The ancient guard-house at l'Eperquerie, Sark, which survived until World War II. It stood on the path between the Militia shooting butts at Le Nez and the picturesque landing place. A family lived there after the Royal Sark Militia was disbanded in 1880.

169. Sark's principal windmill as it appeared about a century ago. It is said to be the oldest tower mill in the British Isles. Its weather vane bears the date of its construction: 1571. Today, the vanes have gone and its tower has been defaced by the Germans, who used it as an observation post. The mill stands 356 feet above sea level.

170. (*below*) In the 1840s it was expected that the silver mines in Little Sark would make a fortune for those who worked them. But these hopes were dashed; the silver veins were weak, costs were high and a valuable cargo worth between £19,000 and £12,000 was lost off the island. Many were ruined, including the Seigneur of Sark, Ernest Le Pelley, who later lost his life in a boating accident. All that remained of the engine house some seventy years ago was this gaunt wall.

171. Quarrying for granite flourished in Herm in about 1815 and persisted for many years. This scene, dating from about 1870, shows one of the quarries on the west coast. Lt. Col. the Hon. John Lindsay and Jonathan Duncan, his son-in-law, had a financial interest at one time in these quarries. Stone was exported to Guernsey (part of St. Peter Port harbour consists of Herm granite) as well as to England, until the trade declined to insignificance in the 1870s.

172. Prince Blücher von Wahlstadt rented Herm from the Crown towards the close of the last century and used this steam launch, the *Marjorie*, to reach the island from Guernsey. Taken in 1904, the picture shows the little vessel off the harbour. The Prince's tenancy was terminated early in the First World War because he was a sub-tenant of the West Bank of Silesia. He was a grandson of the famous Prussian marshal who took part in the campaign at Waterloo in 1815.

173. Herm harbour in about 1870, with the paddle steamer *Rescue I* alongside. She was there on an excursion from Guernsey. The crane on the quay is still there.

174. Herm harbour in 1912. The White House Hotel in the centre was established in the 1870s. The little port was built to provide shelter and accomodation for ships loading granite from the quarries. The island's lock-up — the conical beehive-like structure on the right — was used to incarcerate intoxicated quarrymen at a time when the population was as high as four hundred.

175 & 176. Jethou is the geographical centre of the Channel Islands. From its 268 ft. summit on a clear day all the other islands can be seen. William the Conqueror gave it to his shipmaster, Restald, who later became a monk and in time gave the island to the Abbey of Mont St. Michel. It became Crown property when Henry V seized alien possessions, and still remains so. At one time pirates were hanged from its highest point and it was once rented by a privateer and used as a base for smuggling by another tenant. From time to time it has been open to visitors and was a popular spot when these photographs were taken before the First World War. It was reached from Guernsey by sailing boat, steamer or later by motor launch. Passengers had to be ferried ashore to the wooden landing stage by rowing boat.

177. (right) Landing at Jethou 75 years ago. In those days the s.s. Assistance, seen anchored in La Percée passage, ran excursions to the island and also to Herm, in the background. Today, Jethou is private property.

178. The remains of the Priory of Our Lady of Lihou in about 1910. A medieval religious house, it fell into decay after the Reformation, and the church was almost destroyed in 1793 in order that it should not be of assistance to the French as a landmark for invasion. The causeway leading to this island off Guernsey's west coast survives, but the farmhouse there was devastated by German shells during the Occupation. Substantial remnants of the ruined priory survive to this day.

179. An old cider mill on Lihou Island in 1911. Within the granite circles is a stone cut like a gear-wheel. The racks behind were used for drying seaweed, which was processed into iodine early in the present century.

180. Frenchwomen washing clothes in a *lavoir* at the foot of Prince Albert's Road, St. Peter Port. The picture dates from about 1900. The *lavoir* remains but the custom has gone.

French Washerwomen, Guernsey. Valentines Series

181. Grande Rocque Hotel, in about 1880. Its proprietor was then J. Robilliard. Subsequently it was rebuilt and today is styled Grandes Rocques Hotel.

182. The church of St. Michel du Valle in about 1860. This part of Guernsey, Le Clos du Valle, was separated from its parent by Le Braye du Valle, a stretch of water, until 1806. Benedictine monks established a priory here at a very early date. The building on the left was the feudal court-house of Le Fief St. Michel, which covered about half the island.

183. Cobo in 1880 presented a vastly different scene from today's. The only sign of traffic is an early tricycle (probably the photographer's) in the right foreground. No trees clothe Le Guet's hillside, and not a bungalow is in sight. A few more substantial buildings are visible near the Cobo Hotel.

184. The Trinity House cottages at Torteval which accommodate the keepers manning Les Hanois lighthouse. It came into use in 1862 and lies a mile and a quarter south-west of Pleinmont Point. Much of the area in the photograph is now well wooded and belongs to the National Trust of Guernsey.

185. In about 1865, when this photograph was taken, the mile-long road from St. Peter Port to the Ivy Gates (Les Granges de Beauvoir) was muddy and almost traffic-free. The arches survive but the gas lamp has disappeared.

186. The road to St. Martin's Point. The circular tower was erected in 1816 in memory of Sir John Doyle, who was Lieutenant-Governor from 1803 to 1816 and who was responsible for building the island's major roads during his tenure of office. The pillar was razed during the German Occupation.

187. St. Apolline's chapel, St. Saviour's, in the 1890s. Dedicated to the patron saint of dentists, it was built as a private chapel by Nicholas Henry in 1394 and became associated with the saint as early as 1452. Originally thatched, it was acquired by the States of Guernsey in 1873 and was then being used as a stable. It was the island's first scheduled 'Ancient Monument'.

188.   Saints Bay a century ago, photographed from the Blanchelande fishermen's harbour. The present quay was not yet built, but an earlier haven existed, which was replaced by the present one after it had been destroyed in a gale. One of the men is holding a fine conger. The others have typical fishing-gear with them.

189.   The main interest in this 1890 view of the Fermain Bay Martello tower is that it was one of the earliest photographs to be taken by Charles Toms. The surroundings are less overgrown than they are today and the Pepperpot tower on the clifftop is plainly visible, viewed from the path leading to Jerbourg.

Island
OF
GUERNSEY.

Grande Rocque
Saline Bay
Long Port
Cobo B.
Homet
Homet Barracks
Le Croc
Vason Bay
Doyle's Milit
Richmond Barracks
Perelle Bay
Druids Altar
Le Ree Point
Le Ree Barracks
LIHOU I.
Brock Battery
Doyle's Military Road
St Saviour
Alarm Gu
Rocquaine Bay
Rocquaine Castle
Rocq. H.ᵗ Barracks
St Peter
Pezerie
Torteval
Plemont
Ourquex Point
Mount Herault
Le Tielle
Trinity
Prive
Corbiere